For My Dear  Ainsley

Poetry can make us know.

Write some and let someone

know something

Love always ...

xxxxxx Dad
oooooo

RANDOM HOUSE

TREASURY *of* YEAR-ROUND POEMS

EDITED BY PATRICIA S. KLEIN

RANDOM HOUSE
REFERENCE

New York   Toronto   London   Sydney   Auckland

Please address inquiries about electronic licensing of any products for use on a network, in software, or on CD-ROM to the Sub-sidiary Rights Department, Random House Information Group, fax 212-572-6003.

This book is available at special discounts for bulk purchases for sales promotions or premiums. Special editions, including person-alized covers, excerpts of existing books, and corporate imprints, can be created in large quantities for special needs. For more infor-mation, write to Random House, Inc., Special Markets/Premium Sales, 1745 Broadway, MD 6-2, New York, NY 10019 or e-mail specialmarkets@randomhouse.com.

Library of Congress Cataloging-in-Publication Data is available.

Visit the Random House Reference Web site:
www.randomwords.com

ISBN-10: 0-375-72146-0
ISBN-13: 978-0-375-72146-5

Printed in China

10 9 8 7 6 5 4 3 2 1

CONTENTS

The Months

January brings the snow,
Makes our feet and fingers glow.

February brings the rain,
Thaws the frozen lake again.

March brings breezes loud and shrill,
Stirs the dancing daffodil.

April brings the primrose sweet,
Scatters daisies at our feet.

May brings flocks of pretty lambs,
Skipping by their fleecy dams.

June brings tulips, lilies, roses,
Fills the children's hands with posies.

Hot July brings cooling showers,
Apricots, and gillyflowers.

August brings the sheaves of corn,
Then the harvest home is borne.

Warm September brings the fruit;
Sportsmen then begin to shoot.

Fresh October brings the pheasants;
Then to gather nuts is pleasant.

Dull November brings the blast;
Then the leaves are whirling fast.

Chill December brings the sleet,
Blazing fire, and Christmas treat.

—*Sara Coleridge*

The Seasons

Spring is showery, flowery, bowery.
Summer: hoppy, choppy, poppy.
Autumn: wheezy, sneezy, freezy.
Winter: slippy, drippy, nippy.

—*Anonymous*

JANUARY

The New Year

Who comes dancing over the snow,
    His soft little feet all bare and rosy?
Open the door, though the wild winds blow,
    Take the child in and make him cosy.
Take him in and hold him dear,
He is the wonderful glad New Year.

—*Dinah Maria Mulock Craik*

New Year's Morning

Only a night from old to new!
Only a night, and so much wrought!
The Old Year's heart all weary grew,
But said: "The New Year rest has brought."
The Old Year's hopes its heart laid down,
As in a grave; but trusting, said:
"The blossoms of the New Year's crown
Bloom from the ashes of the dead."
The Old Year's heart was full of greed;
With selfishness it longed and ached,
And cried: "I have not half I need.
My thirst is bitter and unslaked.
But to the New Year's generous hand
All gifts in plenty shall return;
True love it shall understand;
By all ye failures it shall learn.
I have been reckless; it shall be
Quiet and calm and pure of life.
I was a slave; it shall go free,
And find sweet peace where I leave strife."

Only a night from old to new!
Never a night such changes brought.
The Old Year had its work to do;
No New Year miracles are wrought.

Always a night from old to new!
Night and the healing balm of sleep!
Each morn is New Year's morn come true,
Morn of a festival to keep.
All nights are sacred nights to make
Confession and resolve and prayer;
All days are sacred days to wake
New gladness in the sunny air.
Only a night from old to new;
Only a sleep from night to morn.
The new is but the old come true;
Each sunrise sees a new year born.

—*Helen Hunt Jackson*

New Year's Day

Last night, while we were fast asleep,
The old year went away.
It can't come back again because
A new one's come to stay.

—*Rachel Field*

Winter

When icicles hang by the wall
   And Dick the shepherd blows his nail,
And Tom bears logs into the hall,
   And milk comes frozen home in pail;
When blood is nipt, and ways be foul,
Then nightly sings the staring owl
      Tu-whoo!
Tu-whit! tu-whoo! A merry note!
While greasy Joan doth keel the pot.

When all around the wind doth blow,
   And coughing drowns the parson's saw,
And birds sit brooding in the snow,
   And Marian's nose looks red and raw;
When roasted crabs hiss in the bowl—
Then nightly sings the staring owl
      Tu-whoo!
Tu-whit! tu-whoo! A merry note!
While greasy Joan doth keel the pot.

—*William Shakespeare*, Love's Labour's Lost

Winter Fancies

I

Winter without
  And warmth within;
The winds may shout
  And the storm begin;
The snows may pack
  At the window pane,
And the skies grow black,
  And the sun remain
Hidden away
  The livelong day—
But here—in here is the warmth of
      May!

II

Swoop your spitefulest
  Up the flue,
  Wild Winds—do!

What in the world do I care for you?
  O delightfulest
    Weather of all,
    Howl and squall,
And shake the trees till the last leaves
      fall!

III

  The joy one feels,
    In an easy-chair,
  Cocking his heels
    In the dancing air
That wreathes the rim of a roaring
      stove
Whose heat loves better than hearts
      can love,
  Will not permit
    The coldest day
    To drive away
The fire in his blood, and the bliss of it!

IV

Then blow, Winds, blow!
  And rave and shriek,
And snarl and snow,
  Till your breath grows weak—
While here in my room
  I'm as snugly shut
As a glad little worm
  In the heart of a nut!

—*James Whitcomb Riley*

Snow

No breath of wind,
No gleam of sun—
Still the white snow
Whirls softly down—
Twig and bough
And blade and thorn
All in an icy
Quiet, forlorn.
Whispering, rustling,
Through the air
On still and stone,
Roof—everywhere,
It heaps its powdery
Crystal flakes,
Of every tree
A mountain makes;
Till pale and faint
At shut of day

Stoops from the West
One wintry ray,
And, feathered in fire,
Where ghosts the moon,
A robin shrills
His lonely tune.

—*Walter de la Mare*

Jack Frost

The door was shut, as doors should be,
  Before you went to bed last night;
Yet Jack Frost has got in, you see,
  And left your window silver white.

He must have waited till you slept;
  And not a single word he spoke,
But penciled o'er the panes and crept
  Away again before you woke.

And now you cannot see the hills
  Nor fields that stretch beyond the lane;
But there are fairer things than these
  His fingers traced on every pane.

Rocks and castles towering high;
  Hills and dales, and streams and fields;
And knights in armor riding by,
  With nodding plumes and shining shields.

And butterflies with gauzy wings;
   And herds of cows and flocks of sheep;
And fruit and flowers and all the things
   You see when you are sound asleep.

He paints them on the windowpane
   In fairy lines with frozen steam;
And when you wake you see again
   The lovely things you saw in dream.

—*Gabriel Setoun*

Winter Wise

Walk fast in snow, in frost walk slow,
And still as you go tread on your toe;
When frost and snow are both together,
Sit by the fire, and spare shoe leather.

—*Traditional*

FEBRUARY

Winter Nights

Now winter nights enlarge
  The number of their houres,
And clouds their stormes discharge
  Upon the ayrie towres.
Let now the chimneys blaze,
  And cups o'erflow with wine:
Let well-tuned words amaze
  With harmonie divine.
Now yellow waxen lights
  Shall waite on hunny Love,
While youthfull Revels, Masques, and Courtly
    sights
  Sleepes leaden spels remove.

This time doth well dispence
  With lovers' long discourse;
Much speech hath some defence,
  Though beauty no remorse.
All doe not all things well;
  Some measures comely tread,
Some knotted Ridles tell,
  Some Poems smoothly read.

The Summer hath his joyes,
   And Winter his delights;
Though Love and all his pleasures are but toyes,
   They shorten tedious nights.

—*Thomas Campion*

A Valentine

Oh! little loveliest lady mine,
What shall I send for your valentine?
Summer and flowers are far away;
Gloomy old Winter is king to-day;
Buds will not blow, and sun will not shine:
What shall I do for a valentine?

I've searched the gardens all through and
    through
For a bud to tell of my love so true;
But buds are asleep, and blossoms are dead,
And the snow beats down on my poor little head:
So, little loveliest lady mine,
Here is my heart for your valentine!

—*Laura Elizabeth Richards*

Sonnet CXVI

Let me not to the marriage of true minds
Admit impediments. Love is not love
Which alters when it alteration finds,
Or bends with the remover to remove:
O, no! it is an ever-fixed mark
That looks on tempests and is never shaken;
It is the star to every wandering bark,
Whose worth's unknown, although his height
   be taken.
Love's not Time's fool, though rosy lips and
   cheeks
Within his bending sickle's compass come;
Love alters not with his brief hours and weeks,
But bears it out even to the edge of doom.
  If this be error, and upon me prov'd,
  I never writ, nor no man ever lov'd.

—*William Shakespeare*

To His Coy Mistress

Had we but world enough, and time,
This coyness, Lady, were no crime.
We would sit down and think which way
To walk and pass our long love's day;
Thou by the Indian Ganges' side
Shouldst rubies find: I by the tide
Of Humber would complain. I would
Love you ten years before the Flood,
And you should, if you please, refuse
Till the conversion of the Jews.
My vegetable love should grow
Vaster than empires, and more slow;
An hundred years should go to praise
Thine eyes and on thy forehead gaze;
Two hundred to adore each breast:
But thirty thousand to the rest;
An age at least to every part,
And the last age should show your heart;
For, Lady, you deserve this state,
Nor would I love at lower rate.
    But at my back I always hear

Time's winged chariot hurrying near;
And yonder all before us lie
Deserts of vast eternity.
Thy beauty shall no more be found,
Nor, in thy marble vault, shall sound
My echoing song; then worms shall try
That long preserved virginity,
And your quaint honour turn to dust,
And into ashes all my lust:
The grave's a fine and private place,
But none, I think, do there embrace.
   Now therefore, while the youthful hue
Sits on thy skin like morning dew,
And while thy willing soul transpires
At every pore with instant fires,
Now let us sport us while we may,
And now, like amorous birds of prey,
Rather at once our time devour
Than languish in his slow-chapt power.
Let us roll all our strength and all
Our sweetness up into one ball,

And tear our pleasures with rough strife
Thorough the iron gates of life:
Thus, though we cannot make our sun
Stand still, yet we will make him run.

—*Andrew Marvell*

How Do I Love Thee?
Let Me Count the Ways

How do I love thee? Let me count the ways.
I love thee to the depth and breadth and height
My soul can reach, when feeling out of sight
For the ends of Being and ideal Grace.
I love thee to the level of every day's
Most quiet need, by sun and candle-light.
I love thee freely, as men strive for Right;
I love thee purely, as they turn from Praise.
I love thee with a passion put to use
In my old griefs, and with my childhood's faith.
I love thee with a love I seemed to lose
With my lost saints—I love thee with the breath,
Smiles, tears, of all my life!—and, if God choose,
I shall but love thee better after death.

—*Elizabeth Barrett Browning*

Velvet Shoes

Let us walk in the white snow
    In a soundless space;
With footsteps quiet and slow,
    At a tranquil pace,
    Under veils of white lace.

I shall go shod in silk,
    And you in wool,
White as a white cow's milk,
    More beautiful
    Than the breast of a gull.

We shall walk through the still town
    In a windless peace;
We shall step upon white down,
    Upon silver fleece,
    Upon softer than these.

We shall walk in velvet shoes:
    Wherever we go
Silence will fall like dews
    On white silence below.
    We shall walk in the snow.

—*Elinor Wylie*

White Fields

1.

In the winter time we go
Walking in the fields of snow;

Where there is no grass at all;
Where the top of every wall,

Every fence and every tree,
Is as white as white can be.

2.

Pointing out the way we came,
Every one of them the same—

All across the fields there be
Prints in silver filigree;

And our mothers always know,
By our footprints in the snow,

Where the children go.

—*James Stephens*

Snow in the Suburbs

Every branch big with it,
Bent every twig with it;
Every fork like a white web-foot;
Every street and pavement mute:
Some flakes have lost their way, and grope back
upward, when
Meeting those meandering down they turn and
descend again.
The palings are glued together like a wall,
And there is no waft of wind with the fleecy
fall.

A sparrow enters the tree,
Whereon immediately
A snow-lump thrice his own slight size
Descends on him and showers his head
and eyes,
And overturns him,
And near inurns him,

And lights on a nether twig, when its brush
Starts off a volley of other lodging lumps with
    a rush.

  The steps are a blanched slope,
  Up which, with feeble hope,
  A black cat comes, wide-eyed and thin;
    And we take him in.

—*Thomas Hardy*

Stopping by Woods
on a Snowy Evening

Whose woods these are I think I know.
His house is in the village though;
He will not see me stopping here
To watch his woods fill up with snow.

My little horse must think it queer
To stop without a farmhouse near
Between the woods and frozen lake
The darkest evening of the year.

He gives his harness bells a shake
To ask if there is some mistake.
The only other sound's the sweep
Of easy wind and downy flake.

The woods are lovely, dark and deep.
But I have promises to keep,
And miles to go before I sleep,
And miles to go before I sleep.

—*Robert Frost*

February Twilight

I stood beside a hill
  Smooth with new-laid snow,
A single star looked out
  From the cold evening glow.

There was no other creature
  That saw what I could see--
I stood and watched the evening star
  As long as it watched me.

—*Sara Teasdale*

MARCH

On the First of March

On the first of March,
The crows begin to search;
By the first of April,
They are sitting still;
By the first of May,
They've all flown away,
Coming greedy back again
With October's wind and rain.

—*Traditional*

Written in March

While Resting on the Bridge at the Foot of Brother's Water.

The Cock is crowing,
The stream is flowing,
The small birds twitter,
The lake doth glitter,
The green field sleeps in the sun;
The oldest and youngest
Are at work with the strongest;
The cattle are grazing,
Their heads never raising;
There are forty feeding like one!

Like an army defeated
The snow hath retreated,
And now doth fare ill
On the top of the bare hill;

The ploughboy is whooping—anon—anon:
  There's joy in the mountains;
  There's life in the fountains;
  Small clouds are sailing,
  Blue sky prevailing;
The rain is over and gone!

—*William Wordsworth*

When Early March Seems Middle May

When country roads begin to thaw
   In mottled spots of damp and dust,
And fences by the margin draw
   Along the frosty crust
Their graphic silhouettes, I say,
The Spring is coming round this way.

When morning-time is bright with sun
   And keen with wind, and both confuse
The dancing, glancing eyes of one
   With tears that ooze and ooze
And nose-tips weep as well as they,
The Spring is coming round this way.

When suddenly some shadow-bird
   Goes wavering beneath the gaze,
And through the hedge the moan is heard
   Of kine that fain would graze
In grasses new, I smile and say,
The Spring is coming round this way.

When knotted horse-tails are untied,
  And teamsters whistle here and there,
And clumsy mitts are laid aside
  And choppers' hands are bare,
And chips are thick where children play,
The Spring is coming round this way.

When through the twigs the farmer tramps,
  And troughs are chunked beneath the trees,
And fragrant hints of sugar-camps
  Astray in every breeze,—
When early March seems middle May,
The Spring is coming round this way.

When coughs are changed to laughs, and when
  Our frowns melt into smiles of glee,
And all our blood thaws out again
  In streams of ecstasy,
And poets wreak their roundelay,
The Spring is coming round this way.

—*James Whitcombe Riley*

A Little Madness

A little Madness in the Spring
Is wholesome even for the King,
But God be with the Clown—
Who ponders this tremendous scene—
This whole Experiment of Green—
As if it were his own!

—*Emily Dickinson*

St. Patrick's Breastplate

I arise today
Through God's strength to pilot me:
God's might to uphold me,
God's wisdom to guide me,
God's eye to look before me,
God's ear to hear me,
God's word to speak for me,
God's hand to guard me,
God's way to lie before me,
God's shield to protect me,
God's host to save me,
From snares of devils,
From temptations of vices,
From every one who shall wish me ill,
Afar and anear,
Alone and in a multitude.

I summon today all these powers between me
    and those evils,
Against every cruel merciless power that may
    oppose my body and soul,

Against incantations of false prophets,
Against black laws of pagandom,
Against false laws of heretics,
Against craft of idolatry,
Against spells of witches and smiths and
    wizards,
Against every knowledge that corrupts man's
    body and soul.

Christ to shield me today
Against poisoning, against burning,
Against drowning, against wounding,
So there come to me abundance of reward.
Christ with me, Christ before me, Christ
    behind me,
Christ in me, Christ beneath me, Christ
    above me,
Christ on my right, Christ on my left,
Christ when I lie down, Christ when I sit down,
    Christ when I arise,

Christ in the heart of every man who thinks
     of me,
Christ in the mouth of every one who speaks
     of me,
Christ in every eye that sees me,
Christ in every ear that hears me.

—*Traditional*

Danny Boy

Oh Danny boy, the pipes, the pipes are calling
From glen to glen, and down the mountain side
The summer's gone, and all the flowers are
    dying
'Tis you, 'tis you must go and I must bide.
But come ye back when summer's in the
    meadow
Or when the valley's hushed and white with
    snow
'Tis I'll be here in sunshine or in shadow
Oh Danny boy, oh Danny boy, I love you so.

And if you come, when all the flowers are dying
And I am dead, as dead I well may be
You'll come and find the place where I am lying
And kneel and say an "Ave" there for me.

And I shall hear, tho' soft you tread above me
And all my dreams will warm and sweeter be
If you'll not fail to tell me that you love me
I'll simply sleep in peace until you come to me.

I'll simply sleep in peace until you come to me.

—*Frederick Edward Weatherly*

When Irish Eyes Are Smiling

There's a tear in your eye,
And I'm wondering why,
For it never should be there at all.
With such pow'r in your smile,
Sure a stone you'd beguile,
So there's never a teardrop should fall.
When your sweet lilting laughter's
Like some fairy song,
And your eyes twinkle bright as can be;
You should laugh all the while
And all other times smile,
And now, smile a smile for me.

When Irish eyes are smiling,
Sure, 'tis like the morn in Spring.
In the lilt of Irish laughter
You can hear the angels sing.
When Irish hearts are happy,
All the world seems bright and gay.
And when Irish eyes are smiling,
Sure, they steal your heart away.

For your smile is a part
Of the love in your heart,
And it makes even sunshine more bright.
Like the linnet's sweet song,
Crooning all the day long,
Comes your laughter and light.
For the springtime of life
Is the sweetest of all
There is ne'er a real care or regret;
And while springtime is ours
Throughout all of youth's hours,
Let us smile each chance we get.

When Irish eyes are smiling,
Sure, 'tis like the morn in Spring.
In the lilt of Irish laughter
You can hear the angels sing.
When Irish hearts are happy,
All the world seems bright and gay.
And when Irish eyes are smiling,
Sure, they steal your heart away.

—*Chauncey Olcott and George Graff, Jr.*

Green Things Growing

O the green things growing, the green things
    growing,
The faint sweet smell of the green things
    growing!
I should like to live, whether I smile or grieve,
Just to watch the happy life of my green things
    growing.

O the fluttering and the pattering of those green
    things growing!
How they talk each to each, when none of us
    are knowing;
In the wonderful white of the weird moonlight
Or the dim dreamy dawn when the cocks are
    crowing.

I love, I love them so—my green things growing!
And I think that they love me, without false
    showing;
For by many a tender touch, they comfort me
    so much,
With the soft mute comfort of green things
    growing.

And in the rich store of their blossoms glowing
Ten for one I take they're on me bestowing:
Oh, I should like to see, if God's will it may be,
Many, many a summer of my green things
    growing!

But if I must be gathered for the angel's sowing,
Sleep out of sight awhile, like the green things
    growing,
Though dust to dust return, I think I'll
    scarcely mourn,
If I may change into green things growing.

—*Dinah Maria Mulock Craik*

To March

Dear March—Come in—
How glad I am—
I hoped for you before—
Put down your Hat—
You must have walked—
How out of Breath you are—
Dear March, how are you, and the Rest—
Did you leave Nature well—
Oh, March, Come right upstairs with me—
I have so much to tell—

I got your Letter, and the Birds—
The Maples never knew that you were com-
ing—till I called
I declare—how Red their Faces grew—
But March, forgive me—and
All those hills you left for me to Hue—
There was no Purple suitable—
You took it all with you—

Who knocks? That April.
Lock the door—
I will not be pursued—
He stayed away a Year to call
When I am occupied—
But trifles look so trivial
As soon as you have come

That Blame is just as dear as Praise
And Praise as mere as Blame—

—*Emily Dickinson*

Chanson Innocente

in Just-
spring   when the world is mud-
luscious the little
lame balloonman

whistles   far   and wee

and eddieandbill come
running from marbles and
piracies and it's
spring

when the world is puddle-wonderful

the queer
old balloonman whistles
far   and   wee
and bettyandisbel come dancing

from hop-scotch and jump-rope and

it's
spring
and

    the

        goat-footed

balloonMan   whistles
far
and
wee

—*e e cummings*

Evening in a Sugar Orchard

From where I lingered in a lull in March
Outside the sugar-house one night for choice,
I called the fireman with a careful voice
And bade him leave the pan and stoke the arch:
"O fireman, give the fire another stoke,
And send more sparks up chimney with the
    smoke."
I thought a few might tangle, as they did,
Among bare maple boughs, and in the rare
Hill atmosphere not cease to glow,
And so be added to the moon up there.
The moon, though slight, was moon enough
    to show
On every tree a bucket with a lid,
And on black ground a bear-skin rug of snow.
The sparks made no attempt to be the moon.
They were content to figure in the trees
As Leo, Orion, and the Pleiades.
And that was what the boughs were full of soon.

—*Robert Frost*

Pippa's Song

The year's at the spring,
And day's at the morn;
Morning's at seven;
The hillside's dew-pearled;
The lark's on the wing;
The snail's on the thorn;
God's in His heaven—
All's right with the world.

—Robert Browning

Spring Torrents

Will it always be like this until I am dead,
   Every spring must I bear it all again
With the first red haze of the budding maple
    boughs,
   And the first sweet-smelling rain?

Oh I am like a rock in the rising river
   Where the flooded water breaks with a low
    call—
Like a rock that knows the cry of the waters
   And cannot answer at all.

—*Sara Teasdale*

Before the Rain

We knew it would rain, for all the morn
  A spirit on slender ropes of mist
Was lowering its golden buckets down
  Into the vapory amethyst.

Of marshes and swamps and dismal fens—
  Scooping the dew that lay in the flowers,
Dipping the jewels out of the sea,
  To sprinkle them over the land in showers.

We knew it would rain, for the poplars showed
  The white of their leaves, the amber grain
Shrunk in the wind—and the lightning now
  Is tangled in tremulous skeins of rain!

—*Thomas Bailey Aldrich*

After the Rain

The rain has ceased, and in my room
   The sunshine pours an airy flood;
And on the church's dizzy vane
   The ancient cross is bathed in blood.

From out the dripping ivy leaves,
   Antiquely carven, gray and high,
A dormer, facing westward, looks
   Upon the village like an eye.

And now it glimmers in the sun,
   A globe of gold, a disk, a speck;
And in the belfry sits a dove
   With purple ripples on her neck.

—*Thomas Bailey Aldrich*

APRIL

The Four Sweet Months

First, April, she with mellow showers
Opens the way for early flowers;
Then after her comes smiling May,
In a more rich and sweet array;
Next enters June, and brings us more
Gems than those two that went before;
Then (lastly) July comes, and she
More wealth brings in than all those three.

—*Robert Herrick*

The First of April

The first of April, some do say,
Is set apart for All Fools' Day.
But why the people call it so
Nor I, nor they themselves do know.

—*Anonymous*

April's Charms

When April scatters charms of primrose gold
Among the copper leaves in thickets old,
And singing skylarks from the meadows rise,
To twinkle like black stars in sunny skies;

When I can hear the small woodpecker ring
Time on a tree for all the birds that sing;
And hear the pleasant cuckoo, loud and long—
The simple bird that thinks two notes a song;

When I can hear the woodland brook, that could
Not drown a babe, with all his threatening mood;
Upon these banks the violets make their home,
And let a few small strawberry blossoms come;

When I go forth on such a pleasant day,
One breath outdoors takes all my cares away;
It goes like heavy smoke, when flames take hold
Of wood that's green and fill a grate with gold.

—*William Henry Davies*

Rain Song

It is not raining rain to me,
   It's raining daffodils;
In every dimpled drop I see
   Wild flowers on the hills.

A cloud of gray engulfs the day
   And overwhelms the town;
It is not raining rain to me,
   It's raining roses down.

It is not raining rain to me,
   But fields of clover bloom,
Where any buccaneering bee
   May find a bed and room.

A health, then, to the happy,
   A fig for him who frets;
It isn't raining rain to me,
   It's raining violets.

—*Robert Loveman*

April

The roofs are shining from the rain.
  The sparrows twitter as they fly,
And with a windy April grace
  The little clouds go by.
Yet the back-yards are bare and brown
  With only one unchanging tree—
I could not be so sure of Spring
  Save that it sings in me.

—*Sara Teasdale*

City Rain

Rain in the city!
I love to see it fall
Slantwise where the buildings crowd
Red brick and all.
Streets of shiny wetness
Where the taxies go,
With people and umbrellas all
Bobbing to and fro.

Rain in the city!
I love to hear it drip
When I am cosy in my room
Snug as any ship,
With toys spread on the table,
With a picture book or two,
And the rain like a rumbling tomb that sings
Through everything I do.

—*Rachel Field*

Dayenu

If God had brought us out from Egypt
　And not visited them with judgment
Dayenu—It would have been enough.

If God had visited them with judgment
　And not cast down their idols
Dayenu—It would have been enough.

If God had destroyed their idols
　And not slain their firstborn
Dayenu—It would have been enough.

If God had only slain their firstborn
　And not given us their substance
Dayenu—It would have been enough.

If God had just given us their substance
　And not parted the Red Sea for us
Dayenu—It would have been enough.

If God had parted the Red Sea for us
  And not let us walk upon the dry sea bed
Dayenu—It would have been enough.

If God had led us across the dry sea bed
  And not drowned our pursuers in its waters
Dayenu—It would have been enough.

If God had drowned our pursuers in its waters
  And not kept us forty years in the wilderness
Dayenu—It would have been enough.

If God had only kept us forty years in the
    wilderness
  And not fed us with manna
Dayenu—It would have been enough.

If God had just fed us with manna
  And not given us the Sabbath rest
Dayenu—It would have been enough.

If God had given us the Sabbath rest
  And not led us to the foot of Sinai
Dayenu—It would have been enough.

If God had brought us to the foot of Sinai
  And not taught us the Torah
Dayenu—It would have been enough.

If God had taught us the Torah
  And not brought us into Israel
Dayenu—It would have been enough.

If God had brought us into Israel
  And not built the Temple there
Dayenu—It would have been enough.

—*Traditional*

Spirit of the Seder

Our house is cleansed, and we await
The celebration of the eight
Days of Pesach. Girl and boy
Anticipate the feast of joy.

Once again we praise the Giver,
Whose Gift of Gifts was to deliver
Us from Ancient bondage, chains
That scarred the hard Egyptian plains.

Leave no family on its own
To celebrate the Feast alone:
Invite them all to see and hear it.
Share the freedom of the spirit.

—*J. Patrick Lewis*

Go Down Moses

When Israel was in Egypt's land,
  (Let my people go.)
Oppressed so hard they could not stand,
  (Let my people go.)

Chorus:
  Go down Moses
  Way down in Egypt land
  Tell old Pharaoh
  "Let my people go."

"Thus spoke the Lord" bold Moses said,
  (Let my people go.)
"If not I'll smite your firstborn dead."
  (Let my people go.)

Chorus

No more in bondage shall they toil,
  (Let my people go.)
Let them come out with Egypt's spoil,
  (Let my people go.)

Chorus

We need not always weep and mourn,
  (Let my people go.)
And wear these slavery chains forlorn.
  (Let my people go.)

Chorus

Your foes shall not forever stand.
  (Let my people go.)
You shall possess your own good land.
  (Let my people go.)

Chorus

Oh, let us all from bondage flee.
   (Let my people go.)
And soon may all the earth be free.
   (Let my people go.)

Chorus

—*Traditional*

Easter Morning

Surrexit Christus sol verus vespere noctis,
  surgit et hinc domini mystica messis agri.
Nunc vaga puniceis apium plebs laeta labore
  floribus instrepitans poblite mella legit.
Nunc variae volucfres permulcent aethera cantu,
  temperat et pernox nunc philomena melos.
Nunc chorus ecclesiae cantat per cantica Sion,
  alleluia suis centuplicatque tonis.
Tado, pater patriae, caelestis guadia paschae
  percipias meritis limina lucis: ave.

Last night did Christ the Sun rise from the dark,
  The mystic harvest of the fields of God,
And now the little wandering tribes of bees
  Are brawling in the scarlet flowers abroad.
The winds are soft with birdsong; all night long
  Darkling the nightingale her descant told,

And now inside church doors the happy folk
   The Alleluia chant a hundredfold.
O father of thy folk, be thine by right
   The Easter joy, the threshold of the light.

—*Sedulius Scottus*

At Easter Time

The little flowers came through the ground,
    At Easter time, at Easter time;
They raised their heads and looked around,
    At happy Easter time.
And every pretty bud did say,
    "Good people, bless this holy day,
For Christ is risen, the angels say
    At happy Easter time!"

The pure white lily raised its cup,
    At Easter time, at Easter time;
The crocus to the sky looked up
    At happy Easter time.
"We'll hear the song of heaven!" they say;
    "Its glory shines on us today,
Oh! may it shine on us alway,
    At holy Easter time!"

'Twas long and long and long ago,
   That Easter time, that Easter time;
But still the pure white lilies blow
   At happy Easter time.
And still each little flower doth say
   "Good Christians, bless this holy day,
For Christ is risen, the angels say
   At blessed Easter time."

—*Laura E. Richards*

Easter Week

See the land, her Easter keeping,
  Rises as her Maker rose.
Seeds, so long in darkness sleeping,
  Burst at last from winter snows.
Earth with heaven above rejoices;
  Fields and gardens hail the spring;
Shaughs and woodlands ring with voices,
  While the wild birds build and sing.

You, to whom your Maker granted
  Powers to those sweet birds unknown,
Use the craft by God implanted;
  Use the reason not your own.
Here, while heaven and earth rejoices,
  Each his Easter tribute bring—
Work of fingers, chant of voices,
  Like the birds who build and sing.

—*Charles Kingsley*

Easter

The air is like a butterfly
With frail blue wings.
The happy earth looks at the sky
And sings.

—*Joyce Kilmer*

End of Winter

Bare-handed reach
to catch
April's
incoming curve.
      Leap
           higher than you thought you could
              and
Hold:
      Spring,
      Solid,
      Here.

—*Eve Merriam*

Take Me Out to the Ball Game

Katie Casey was base ball mad.
Had the fever and had it bad;
Just to root for the home town crew,
Ev'ry sound Katie blew.
On a Saturday, her young beau
Called to see if she'd like to go,
To see a show but Miss Kate said,
"No, I'll tell you what you can do."

"Take me out to the ball game,
Take me out with the crowd.
Buy me some peanuts and cracker jack,
I don't care if I never get back,
Let me root, root, root for the home team,
If they don't win it's a shame.
For it's one, two, three strikes, you're out,
At the old ball game."

Katie Casey saw all the games,
Knew the players by their first names;
Told the umpire he was wrong,
All along good and strong.
When the score was just two to two,
Katie Casey knew what to do,
Just to cheer up the boys she knew,
She made the gang sing this song:

"Take me out to the ball game,
Take me out with the crowd.
Buy me some peanuts and cracker jack,
I don't care if I never get back,
Let me root, root, root for the home team,
If they don't win it's a shame.
For it's one, two, three strikes, you're out,
At the old ball game."

—*Jack Norworth*

MAY

May Day

A delicate fabric of bird song
  Floats in the air,
The smell of wet wild earth
  Is everywhere.

Red small leaves of the maple
  Are clenched like a hand,
Like girls at their first communion
  The pear trees stand.

Oh I must pass nothing by
  Without loving it much,
The raindrop try with my lips,
  The grass with my touch;

For how can I be sure
  I shall see again
The world on the first of May
  Shining after the rain?

—*Sara Teasdale*

Phases of the Moon

Once upon a time I heard
That the flying moon was a Phoenix bird;
Thus she sails through windy skies,
Thus in the willow's arms she lies;
Turn to the East or turn to the West
In many trees she makes her nest.
When she's but a pearly thread
Look among birch leaves overhead;
When she dies in yellow smoke
Look in a thunder-smitten oak;
But in May when the moon is full,
Bright as water and white as wool,
Look for her where she loves to be,
Asleep in a high magnolia tree.

—*Elinor Wylie*

Here We Come A-Piping

Here we come a-piping,
In Springtime and in May;
Green fruit a-ripening,
And Winter fled away.
The Queen she sits upon the strand,
Fair as lily, white as wand;
Seven billows on the sea,
Horses riding fast and free,
And bells beyond the sand.

—*Anonymous*

A Prayer in Spring

Oh, give us pleasure in the flowers today;
And give us not to think so far away
As the uncertain harvest; keep us here
All simply in the springing of the year.

Oh, give us pleasure in the orchard white,
Like nothing else by day, like ghosts by night;
And make us happy in the happy bees,
The swarm dilating round the perfect trees.

And make us happy in the darting bird
That suddenly above the bees is heard,
The meteor that thrusts in with needle bill,
And off a blossom in mid-air stands still.

For this is love and nothing else is love,
To which it is reserved for God above
To sanctify to what far ends He will,
But which it only needs that we fulfill.

—*Robert Frost*

There Is But One May in the Year

There is but one May in the year,
And sometimes May is wet and cold;
There is but one May in the year
Before the year grows old.

Yet though it be the chilliest May,
With least of sun and most of showers,
Its wind and dew, its night and day,
Bring up the flowers.

—*Christina Rossetti*

Piano

Softly, in the dusk, a woman is singing to me;
Taking me back down the vista of years, till I
    see
A child sitting under the piano, in the boom of
    the tingling strings
And pressing the small, poised feet of a mother
    who smiles as she sings.

In spite of myself, the insidious mastery of song
Betrays me back, till the heart of me weeps to
    belong
To the old Sunday evenings at home, with
    winter outside
And hymns in the cosy parlour, the tinkling
    piano our guide.

So now it is vain for the singer to burst into
    clamour
With the great black piano appassionato. The
    glamour
Of childish days is upon me, my manhood is cast
Down in the flood of remembrance, I weep like
    a child for the past.

—*D. H. Lawrence*

"I Love You"

"I love you,"
said a great mother.
"I love you for what you are
knowing so well what you are.
And I love you more yet, child,
deeper yet than ever, child,
for what you are going to be,
knowing so well you are going far,
knowing your great works are ahead,
ahead and beyond,
yonder and far over yet."

—Carl Sandburg, from "The People, Yes"

The Courage That My Mother Had

The courage that my mother had
Went with her, and is with her still:
Rock from New England quarried;
Now granite in a granite hill.

The golden brooch my mother wore
She left behind for me to wear;
I have no thing I treasure more:
Yet, it is something I could spare.

Oh, if instead she'd left to me
The thing she took into the grave!—
That courage like a rock, which she
Has no more need of, and I have.

—*Edna St. Vincent Millay*

The Adversary

Mothers are hardest to forgive.
Life is the fruit they long to hand you,
Ripe on a plate. And while you live,
Relentlessly they understand you.

—*Phyllis McGinley*

Night and Morning

The morning sits outside afraid
Until my mother draws the shade;

Then it bursts in like a ball,
Splashing sun all up the wall.

And the evening is not night
Until she's tucked me in just right
And kissed me and turned out the light.

Oh, if my mother went away
Who would start the night and day?

—*Dorothy Aldis*

Decoration Day

Sleep, comrades, sleep and rest
   On this Field of the Grounded Arms,
Where foes no more molest,
   Nor sentry's shot alarms!

Ye have slept on the ground before,
   And started to your feet
At the cannon's sudden roar,
   Or the drum's redoubling beat.

But in this camp of Death
   No sound your slumber breaks;
Here is no fevered breath,
   No wound that bleeds and aches.

All is repose and peace,
   Untrampled lies the sod;
The shouts of battle cease,
   It is the Truce of God!

Rest, comrades, rest and sleep!
  The thoughts of men shall be
As sentinels to keep
  Your rest from danger free.

Your silent tents of green
  We deck with fragrant flowers;
Yours has the suffering been,
  The memory shall be ours.

—*Henry Wadsworth Longfellow*

When Johnny Comes Marching Home Again

When Johnny comes marching home again,
   Hurrah! Hurrah!
We'll give him a hearty welcome then,
   Hurrah! Hurrah!
The men will cheer, the boys will shout,
The ladies they will all turn out,
   And we'll all feel gay
When Johnny comes marching home.

The old church bell will peal with joy,
   Hurrah! Hurrah!
To welcome home our darling boy,
   Hurrah! Hurrah!
The village lads and lassies say
With roses they will strew the way,
   And we'll all feel gay
When Johnny comes marching home.

Get ready for the Jubilee,
    Hurrah! Hurrah!
We'll give the hero three times three,
    Hurrah! Hurrah!
The laurel wreath is ready now
To place upon his loyal brow,
    And we'll all feel gay
When Johnny comes marching home.

—*Traditional*

The Blue and the Gray

By the flow of the inland river,
  Whence the fleets of iron have fled,
Where the blades of the grave-grass quiver,
  Asleep are the ranks of the dead;—
    Under the sod and the dew,
      Waiting the judgment-day;—
    Under the one, the Blue;
      Under the other, the Gray.

These in the robings of glory,
  Those in the gloom of defeat,
All with the battle-blood gory,
  In the dusk of eternity meet;—
    Under the sod and the dew,
      Waiting the judgment-day;—
    Under the laurel, the Blue;
      Under the willow, the Gray.

From the silence of sorrowful hours
  The desolate mourners go,
Lovingly laden with flowers
  Alike for the friend and the foe;—

Under the sod and the dew,
    Waiting the judgment-day;—
Under the roses, the Blue;
    Under the lilies, the Gray.

So with an equal splendor
  The morning sun-rays fall,
With a touch, impartially tender,
  On the blossoms blooming for all;
    Under the sod and the dew,
        Waiting the judgment-day;—
    Broidered with gold, the Blue;
        Mellowed with gold, the Gray.

So, when the summer calleth,
  On forest and field of grain
With an equal murmur falleth
  The cooling drip of the rain;—
    Under the sod and the dew,
        Waiting the judgment-day;—
    Wet with the rain, the Blue,
        Wet with the rain, the Gray.

Sadly, but not with upbraiding,
　The generous deed was done;
In the storm of the years that are fading
　No braver battle was won;—
　　Under the sod and the dew,
　　　Waiting the judgment-day;—
　　Under the blossoms, the Blue;
　　　Under the garlands, the Gray.

No more shall the war-cry sever,
　Or the winding rivers be red;
They banish our anger forever
　When they laurel the graves of our dead!
　　Under the sod and the dew,
　　　Waiting the judgment-day;—
　　Love and tears for the Blue;
　　　Tears and love for the Gray.

—*Francis Miles Finch*

Spring in War Time

I feel the spring far off, far off,
  The faint far scent of bud and leaf—
Oh, how can Spring take heart to come
  To a world in grief,
  Deep grief?

The sun turns north, the days grow long,
  Later the evening star grows bright—
How can the daylight linger on
  For men to fight,
  Still fight?

The grass is waking in the ground,
  Soon it will rise and blow in waves—
How can it have the heart to sway
  Over the graves,
  New graves?

Under the boughs where lovers walked
    The apple-blooms will shed their breath—
But what of all the lovers now
    Parted by Death,
    Grey Death?

—*Sara Teasdale*

JUNE

The Days Are Clear

The days are clear,
Day after day,
When April's here,
That leads to May,
And June
Must follow soon:
Stay, June stay!—
If only we could stop the moon
And June!

—*Christina Rossetti*

The School-Boy

I love to rise in a summer morn,
When the birds sing on every tree;
The distant huntsman winds his horn,
And the sky-lark sings with me.
O! what sweet company.

But to go to school in a summer morn,
O! it drives all joy away;
Under a cruel eye outworn,
The little ones spend the day
In sighing and dismay.

Ah! then at times I drooping sit,
And spend many an anxious hour,
Nor in my book can I take delight,
Nor sit in learning's bower,
Worn thro' with the dreary shower.

How can the bird that is born for joy
Sit in a cage and sing?
How can a child, when fears annoy,
But droop his tender wing,
And forget his youthful spring?

O! father and mother, if buds are nip'd
And blossoms blown away,
And if the tender plants are strip'd
Of their joy in the springing day,
By sorrow and care's dismay,

How shall the summer arise in joy,
Or the summer fruits appear?
Or how shall we gather what griefs destroy,
Or bless the mellowing year,
When the blasts of winter appear?

—*William Blake*

Bed in Summer

In winter I get up at night
And dress by yellow candle-light.
In summer quite the other way,
I have to go to bed by day.

I have to go to bed and see
The birds still hopping on the tree,
Or hear the grown-up people's feet
Still going past me in the street.

And does it not seem hard to you,
When all the sky is clear and blue,
And I should like so much to play,
To have to go to bed by day?

—*Robert Louis Stevenson*

Parental Ode to My Son, Aged Three Years and Five Months

Thou happy, happy elf!
(But stop,—first let me kiss away that tear!)—
Thou tiny image of myself!
(My love, he's poking peas into his ear!)
Thou merry, laughing sprite,
With spirits feather-light,
Untouched by sorrow, and unsoiled by sin—
(Good heavens! the child is swallowing a pin!)

Thou little tricksy Puck!
With antic toys so funnily bestuck,
Light as the singing bird that wings the air—
(The door! the door! he'll tumble down the stair!)
Thou darling of thy sire!
(Why, Jane, he'll set his pinafore afire!)
Thou imp of mirth and joy!
In love's dear chain, so strong and bright a link,
Thou idol of thy parents—(Drat the boy!
There goes my ink!)

Thy father's pride and hope!
(He'll break the mirror with that skipping-rope!)
With pure heart newly stamped from Nature's
    mint—
(Where *did* he learn that squint?)
  Thou young domestic dove!
(He'll have that jug off with another shove!)
  Dear nursling of the hymeneal nest!
  (Are these torn clothes his best?)
  Little epitome of man!
(He'll climb upon the table, that's his plan!)
Touched with the beauteous tints of dawning life
  (He's got a knife!)

  Thou pretty opening rose!
(Go to your mother, child, and wipe your nose!)
Balmy and breathing music like the South,
(He really brings my heart into my mouth!)

Fresh as the morn, and brilliant as its star,—
(I wish that window had an iron bar!)
Bold as the hawk, yet gentle as the dove,—
    (I'll tell you what, my love,
I cannot write unless he's sent above!)

—*Thomas Hood*

Epigrams: On my First Son

Farewell, thou child of my right hand, and joy;
My sin was too much hope of thee, lov'd boy.
Seven years tho' wert lent to me, and I thee pay,
Exacted by thy fate, on the just day.
O, could I lose all father now! For why
Will man lament the state he should envy?
To have so soon 'scap'd world's and flesh's rage,
And if no other misery, yet age?
Rest in soft peace, and, ask'd, say, "Here doth lie
Ben Jonson his best piece of poetry."
For whose sake henceforth all his vows be such,
As what he loves may never like too much.

—*Ben Jonson*

June

Strong June, superb, serene, elate
With conscience of thy sovereign state
Untouched of thunder, though the storm
Scathe here and there thy shuddering skies
And bid its lightning cross thine eyes
With fire, thy golden hours inform
Earth and the souls of men with life
That brings forth peace from shining strife.

—*Algernon Charles Swinburne*

Cornish Midsummer Bonfire Song

The bonny month of June is crowned
With the sweet scarlet rose;
The groves and meadows all around
With lovely pleasure flows.

As I walked out to yonder green,
One evening so fair;
All where the fair maids may be seen
Playing at the bonfire.

Hail! lovely nymphs, be not too coy,
But freely yield your charms;
Let love inspire with mirth and joy,
In Cupid's lovely arms.

Bright Luna spreads its light around,
The gallants for to cheer;
As they lay sporting on the ground,
At the fair June bonfire.

All on the pleasant dewy mead,
They shared each other's charms;
Till Phoebus' beams began to spread,
And coming day alarms.

Whilst larks and linnets sing so sweet,
To cheer each lovely swain;
Let each prove true unto their love,
And so farewell the plain.

—*Traditional*

Daisies

Over the shoulders and slopes of the dune
I saw the white daisies go down to the sea,
A host in the sunshine, an army in June,
The people God sends us to set our hearts free.

The bobolinks rallied them up from the dell,
The orioles whistled them out of the wood;
And all of their singing was, "Earth, it is well!"
And all of their dancing was, "Life, thou art
    good!"

—*Bliss Carman*

Dusk in June

Evening, and all the birds
  In a chorus of shimmering sound
Are easing their hearts of joy
  For miles around.

The air is blue and sweet,
  The few first stars are white,—
Oh let me like the birds
  Sing before night.

—*Sara Teasdale*

JULY

Here's to July

Here's to July.
For the bird,
And the bee,
And the butterfly;
For the flowers
That blossom
For feasting the eye;
For skates, balls,
And jump ropes,
For swings that go high;
For rocketry
Fireworks that
Blaze in the sky,
Oh, here's to July.

—*Anonymous*

Fourth of July Parade

Hear the blare of bugles,
Hear the beat of drums,
Hear the sound of marching feet.
Down the street there comes,
   Playing, marching,
   Marching, playing,
   In the sun and shade,
   All the music,
   All the color,
   Of the Fourth's parade.

See the buglers blowing,
See the drummers pound,
See the feet go up and down
To the music's sound.
   Playing, marching,
   Marching, playing,
   In the shade and sun,
   All the color,
   All the music,
   Says the Fourth's begun.

—*Anonymous*

Independence Day, 1941

This is Independence Day,
Fourth of July, the day we mean to keep,
Whatever happens and whatever falls
Out of a sky grown strange;
This is firecracker day for sunburnt kids,
The day of the parade,
Slambanging down the street.
Listen to the parade!
There's J. K. Burney's float,
Red-white-and-blue crepe-paper on the wheels,
The Fire Department and the local Grange,
There are the pretty girls with their hair curled
Who represent the Thirteen Colonies,
The Spirit of East Greenwich, Betsy Ross,
Democracy, or just some pretty girls.
There are the veterans and the Legion Post
(Their feet are going to hurt when they get
    home).
The band, the flag, the band, the usual crowd,
Good-humored, watching, hot,

Silent a second as the flag goes by,
Kidding the local cop and eating popsicles,
Jack Brown and Rosie Shapiro and Dan Shay,
Paul Bunchick and the Greek who runs the
    Greek's,
The black-eyed children out of Sicily,
The girls who giggle and the boys who push,
All of them there and all of them a nation.
And, afterwards,
There'll be ice-cream and fireworks and a speech
By somebody the Honorable Who,
The lovers will pair off in the kind dark
And Tessie Jones, our honor-graduate,
Will read the declaration.
That's how it is. It's always been that way.
That's our Fourth of July, through war and peace,
That's our Fourth of July.

—*Stephen Vincent Benet*

The Star-Spangled Banner

Oh, say can you see, by the dawn's early light,
   What so proudly we hailed at the twilight's
      last gleaming,
Whose broad stripes and bright stars, through
      the perilous fight,
   O'er the ramparts we watched, were so
      gallantly streaming?
And the rockets' red glare, the bombs bursting
      in air,
Gave proof through the night that our flag was
      still there.
O say, does that star-spangled banner yet wave
O'er the land of the free, and the home of the
      brave!

On the shore, dimly seen through the mists of
      the deep,
   Where the foe's haughty host in dread silence
      reposes,
What is that which the breeze, o'er the
      towering steep,
   As it fitfully blows, half conceals, half discloses?

Now it catches the gleam of the morning's first
    beam,
In full glory reflected, now shines on the stream.
'Tis the star-spangled banner; oh, long may it
    wave
O'er the land of the free, and the home of the
    brave!

And where is that band who so vauntingly
    swore
  That the havoc of war and the battle's
    confusion
A home and a country should leave us no more?
  Their blood has wiped out their foul
    footsteps' pollution.
No refuge could save the hireling and slave
From the terror of flight, or the gloom of the
    grave:
And the star-spangled banner in triumph doth
    wave
O'er the land of the free, and the home of the
    brave.

Oh! thus be it ever when freemen shall stand
  Between their loved homes and the war's
    desolation;
Blest with victory and peace, may the
    heaven-rescued land
  Praise the Power that hath made and
    preserved us a nation!
Then conquer we must, when our cause it is just,
And this be our motto: "In God is our trust!"
And the star-spangled banner in triumph doth
    wave,
O'er the land of the free, and the home of the
    brave!

—*Francis Scott Key*

The New Colossus

Not like the brazen giant of Greek fame,
With conquering limbs astride from land to land;
Here at our sea-washed, sunset gates shall stand
A mighty woman with a torch, whose flame
Is the imprisoned lightning, and her name
Mother of Exiles. From her beacon-hand
Glows world-wide welcome; her mild eyes command
The air-bridged harbor that twin cities frame.
"Keep, ancient lands, your storied pomp!" cries she
With silent lips. "Give me your tired, your poor,
Your huddled masses yearning to breathe free,
The wretched refuse of your teeming shore.
Send these, the homeless, tempest-tost to me,
I lift my lamp beside the golden door!"

—*Emma Lazarus*

America the Beautiful

O beautiful for spacious skies,
  For amber waves of grain,
For purple mountains majesties
  Above the fruited plain!
America! America!
  God shed His grace on thee
And crown thy good with brotherhood
  From sea to shining sea!

O beautiful for pilgrim feet,
  Whose stern, impassioned stress
A thoroughfare for freedom beat
  Across the wilderness!
America! America!
  God mend thine every flaw,
Confirm thy soul in self-control,
  Thy liberty in law!

O beautiful for heroes proved
  In liberating strife,
Who more than self their country loved,
  And mercy more than life!

America! America!
  May God thy gold refine,
Till all success be nobleness
  And every gain divine!

O beautiful for patriot dream
  That sees beyond the years
Thine alabaster cities gleam
  Undimmed by human tears!
America! America!
  God shed His grace on thee,
And crown thy good with brotherhood
  From sea to shining sea!

—*Katharine Lee Bates*

July

There is a month between the swath and sheaf
When grass is gone
And corn still grassy;
When limes are massy
With hanging leaf,
And pollen-coloured blooms whereon
Bees are voices we can hear,
So hugely dumb
This silent month of the attaining year.
The white-faced roses slowly disappear
From field and hedgerow, and no more flowers
    come;
Earth lies in strain of powers
Too terrible for flowers:
And, would we know
Her burden, we must go

Forth from the vale, and, ere the sunstrokes
    slacken,
Stand at a moorland's edge and gaze
Across the hush and blaze
Of the clear-burning, verdant summer bracken;
For in that silver flame
Is writ July's own name—
The ineffectual, numbed sweet
Of passion at its heat.

—*Michael Field*

Summer Stars

Bend low again, night of summer stars.
So near you are, sky of summer stars,
So near, a long-arm man can pick off stars,
Pick off what he wants in the sky bowl,
So near you are, summer stars,
So near, strumming, strumming,
   So lazy and hum-strumming.

—*Carl Sandburg*

Summer Sun

Great is the sun, and wide he goes
Through empty heaven without repose;
And in the blue and glowing days
More thick than rain he showers his rays.

Though closer still the blinds we pull
To keep the shady parlour cool,
Yet he will find a chink or two
To slip his golden fingers through.

The dusty attic spider-clad,
He, through the keyhole, maketh glad;
And through the broken edge of tiles
Into the laddered hay-loft smiles.

Meantime his golden face around
He bares to all the garden ground,
And sheds a warm and glittering look
Among the ivy's inmost nook.

Above the hills, along the blue,
Round the bright air with footing true,
To please the child, to paint the rose,
The gardener of the World, he goes.

—*Robert Louis Stevenson*

AUGUST

August

The sprinkler twirls.
  The summer wanes.
The pavement wears
  Popsicle stains.

The playground grass
  Is worn to dust.
The weary swings
  Creak, creak with rust.

The trees are bored
  With being green.
Some people leave
  The local scene

And go to seaside
  Bungalows
And take off nearly
  All their clothes.

—*John Updike*

A Boat Beneath a Sunny Sky

A boat beneath a sunny sky,
Lingering onward dreamily
In an evening of July—

Children three that nestle near,
Eager eye and willing ear,
Pleased a simple tale to hear—

Long has paled that sunny sky:
Echoes fade and memories die:
Autumn frosts have slain July.

Still she haunts me, phantomwise,
Alice moving under skies
Never seen by waking eyes.

Children yet, the tale to hear,
Eager eye and willing ear,
Lovingly shall nestle near.

In a Wonderland they lie,
Dreaming as the days go by,
Dreaming as the summers die:

Ever drifting down the stream—
Lingering in the golden gleam—
Life, what is it but a dream?

—*Lewis Carroll*

August Moonlight

The solemn light behind the barns,
　　The rising moon, the cricket's call,
The August night, and you and I—
　　What is the meaning of it all!

Has it a meaning, after all?
　　Or is it one of Nature's lies,
That net of beauty that she casts
　　Over Life's unsuspecting eyes?

That web of beauty that she weaves
　　For one strange purpose of her own,—
For this the painted butterfly,
　　For this the rose—for this alone!

Strange repetition of the rose,
　　And strange reiterated call
Of bird and insect, man and maid,—
　　Is that the meaning of it all?

If it means nothing after all!
  And nothing lives except to die—
It is enough—that solemn light
  Behind the barns, and you and I.

—*Richard Le Gallienne*

The Rainy Summer

There's much afoot in heaven and earth this year;
  The winds hunt up the sun, hunt up the moon,
Trouble the dubious dawn, hasten the drear
  Height of a threatening noon.

No breath of boughs, no breath of leaves, of
    fronds,
  May linger or grow warm; the trees are loud;
The forest, rooted, tosses in her bonds,
  And strains against the cloud.

No scents may pause within the garden-fold;
  The rifled flowers are cold as ocean-shells;
Bees, humming in the storm, carry their cold
  Wild honey to cold cells.

—*Alice Meynell*

Rain in Summer

How beautiful is the rain!
After the dust and heat,
In the broad and fiery street,
In the narrow lane,
How beautiful is the rain!
How it clatters along the roofs
Like the tramp of hoofs!

How it gushes and struggles out
From the throat of the overflowing spout!
Across the window pane
It pours and pours;
And swift and wide,
With a muddy tide,
Like a river down the gutter roars
The rain, the welcome rain!

—*Henry Wadsworth Longfellow*

Summer

Rushes in a watery place,
　　And reeds in a hollow;
A soaring skylark in the sky,
　　A darting swallow;
And where pale blossom used to hang
　　Ripe fruit to follow.

—*Christina Rossetti*

In August

From the great trees the locusts cry
In quavering ecstatic duo—a boy
Shouts a wild call—a mourning dove
In the blue distance sobs—the wind
Wanders by, heavy with odors
Of corn and wheat and melon vines;
The trees tremble with delirious joy as the
    breeze
Greets them, one by one—now the oak,
Now the great sycamore, now the elm.

And the locusts in brazen chorus, cry
Like stricken things, and the ring-dove's note
Sobs on in the dim distance.

—*Hamlin Garland*

In August

Heat urges secret odors from the grass.
Blunting the edge of silence, crickets shrill.
Wings veer: inane needles of light, and pass.
Laced pools: the warm wood-shadows ebb and
    fill.
The wind is casual, loitering to crush
The sun upon his palate, and to draw
Pungence from pine, frank fragrances from
    brush,
Sucked up through thin grey boughs as through
    a straw.

Moss-green, fern-green and leaf and
    meadow-green
Are broken by the bare, bone-colored roads,
Less moved by stirring air than by unseen
Soft-footed ants and meditative toads.
Summer is passing, taking what she brings:
Green scents and sounds, and quick ephemeral
    wings.

—*Babette Deutsch*

August

Buttercup nodded and said good-by,
Clover and daisy went off together,
But the fragrant water lilies lie
Yet moored in the golden August weather.

The swallows chatter about their flight,
The cricket chirps like a rare good fellow,
The asters twinkle in clusters bright,
While the corn grows ripe and the apples mellow.

—*Celia Thaxter*

Summer

Winter is cold-hearted,
　　Spring is yea and nay,
Autumn is a weathercock
Blown every way.
　　Summer days for me
When every leaf is on its tree;

When Robin's not a beggar,
　　And Jenny Wren's a bride,
And larks hang singing, singing, singing,
　　Over the wheat-fields wide,
　　And anchored lilies ride,
And the pendulum spider
　　Swings from side to side,

And blue-black beetles transact business,
　　And gnats fly in a host,
And furry caterpillars hasten
　　That no time be lost,
And moths grow fat and thrive,
And ladybirds arrive.

Before green apples blush,
  Before green nuts embrown,
Why, one day in the country
Is worth a month in town;
  Is worth a day and a year
Of the dusty, musty, lag-last fashion
  That days drone elsewhere.

—*Christina Rossetti*

Summer and Autumn

The hot mid-summer, the bright mid-summer
Reigns in its glory now:
The earth is scorched with a golden fire,
There are berries, dead-ripe, on every brier,
And fruits on every bough.

But the autumn days, so sober and calm,
Steeped in a dreamy haze,
When the uplands all with harvests shine,
And we drink the wind like a fine cool wine—
Ah, those are the best of days!

—*Richard Henry Stoddard*

SEPTEMBER

Robin Redbreast

Good-bye, good-bye to Summer!
For Summer's nearly done;
The garden smiling faintly,
Cool breezes in the sun;
Our Thrushes now are silent,
Our Swallows flown away,—
But Robin's here, in coat of brown,
With ruddy breast-knot gay.
Robin, Robin Redbreast,
O Robin dear!
Robin singing sweetly
In the falling of the year.

Bright yellow, red, and orange,
The leaves come down in hosts;
The trees are Indian Princes,
But soon they'll turn to Ghosts;
The scanty pears and apples
Hang russet on the bough,
It's Autumn, Autumn, Autumn late,
'Twill soon be Winter now.

Robin, Robin Redbreast,
O Robin dear!
And welaway! my Robin,
For pinching times are near.

The fireside for the Cricket,
The wheatstack for the Mouse,
When trembling night-winds whistle
And moan all round the house;
The frosty ways like iron,
The branches plumed with snow,—
Alas! in Winter, dead and dark,
Where can poor Robin go?
Robin, Robin Redbreast,
O Robin dear!
And a crumb of bread for Robin,
His little heart to cheer.

—*William Allingham*

Autumn

The morns are meeker than they were—
The nuts are getting brown—
The berry's cheek is plumper—
The Rose is out of town.

The maple wears a gayer scarf—
The field a scarlet gown—
Lest I should be old-fashioned
I'll put a trinket on.

—*Emily Dickinson*

September

The dark green Summer, with its massive hues,
Fades into Autumn's tincture manifold.
A gorgeous garniture of fire and gold
The high slope of the ferny hill indues.
The mists of morn in slumbering layers diffuse
O'er glimmering rock, smooth lake, and spiked
    array
Of hedge-row thorns, a unity of grey.
All things appear their tangible form to lose
In ghostly vastness. But anon the gloom
Melts, as the Sun puts off his muddy veil;
And now the birds their twittering songs
    resume,
All Summer silent in the leafy dale.
In Spring they piped of love on every tree,
But now they sing the song of memory.

—*Hartley Coleridge*

Psalm of Those Who Go Forth Before Daylight

The policeman buys shoes slow and careful; the
    teamster buys gloves slow and careful; they
    take care of their feet and hands; they live
    on their feet and hands.

The milkman never argues; he works alone and
    no one speaks to him; the city is asleep when
    he is on the job; he puts a bottle on six
    hundred porches and calls it a day's work; he
    climbs two hundred wooden stairways; two
    horses are company for him; he never argues.

The rolling-mill men and the sheet-steel men
    are brothers of cinders; they empty cinders
    out of their shoes after the day's work; they
    ask their wives to fix burnt holes in the
    knees of their trousers; their necks and ears
    are covered with a smut; they scour their
    necks and ears; they are brothers of cinders.

—*Carl Sandburg*

I Hear America Singing

I hear America singing, the varied carols I hear;
Those of mechanics—each one singing his,
    as it should be, blithe and strong;
The carpenter singing his, as he measures his
    plank or beam,
The mason singing his, as he makes ready for
    work, or leaves off work;
The boatman singing what belongs to him in
    his boat—the deckhand singing on the
    steamboat deck;
The shoemaker singing as he sits on his
    bench—the hatter singing as he stands;
The woodcutter's song—the ploughboy's,
    on his way in the morning, or at noon
    intermission, or at sundown;

The delicious singing of the mother—or of the
    young wife at work—or of the girl sewing
    or washing—
Each singing what belongs to him or her,
    and to none else;
The day what belongs to the day—At night,
    the party of young fellows, robust, friendly,
Singing, with open mouths, their strong
    melodious songs.

—*Walt Whitman*

Labor Day

The elderberries explain
  the generation holding on.
A neighbor drops off
  two bushel of handpicked fruit,
    wild and free as the queen's white lace.
Mother groans at the tasteless treasure,
  bird seed in royal hue.
She's worked a tired week,
  putting up worthy fare, corn and pear.
And with tomatoes turning, trash 'em.
Dad will not bury a berry.
Gathered, we younger help him
  strip the clusters, perfectly ripe.

While we sleep, he finishes one basket,
  dents the other.
By noon Mother stacks
  the freezer shelf with pints
  of purple pellets, filler for muffins,
  breakfast stew, and Christmas pies
  spruced with lemon and peaches.
The gift is accepted,
  the storehouse lined.
The winter is coming,
  provision supplied.

—*Evelyn Bence*

First Day of School

I wonder
if my drawing
will be as good as theirs.
I wonder
if they'll like me
or just be full of stares.
I wonder
if my teacher
will look like Mom or Gram.
I wonder
if my puppy
will wonder
where I am!

—*Aileen Fisher*

On an Apple-Ripe September Morning

On an apple-ripe September morning
Through the mist-chill fields I went
With a pitch-fork on my shoulder
Less for use than for devilment.

The threshing mill was set-up, I knew,
In Cassidy's haggard last night,
And we owed them a day at the threshing
Since last year. O it was delight

To be paying bills of laughter
And chaffy gossip in kind
With work thrown in to ballast
The fantasy-soaring mind.

As I crossed the wooden bridge I wondered
As I looked into the drain
If ever a summer morning should find me
Shovelling up eels again.

And I thought of the wasps' nest in the bank
And how I got chased one day
Leaving the drag and the scraw-knife behind,
How I covered my face with hay.

The wet leaves of the cocksfoot
Polished my boots as I
Went round by the glistening bog-holes
Lost in unthinking joy.

I'll be carrying bags to-day, I mused,
The best job at the mill
With plenty of time to talk of our loves
As we wait for the bags to fill.

Maybe Mary might call round . . .
And then I came to the haggard gate,
And I knew as I entered that I had come
Through fields that were part of no earthly estate.

—*Patrick Kavanagh*

September

The golden-rod is yellow;
  The corn is turning brown;
The trees in apple orchards
  With fruit are bending down.

The gentian's bluest fringes
  Are curling in the sun;
In dusty pods the milkweed
  Its hidden silk has spun.

The sedges flaunt their harvest,
  In every meadow nook;
And asters by the brook-side
  Make asters in the brook.

From dewy lanes at morning
  The grapes' sweet odors rise;
At noon the roads all flutter
  With yellow butterflies.

By all these lovely tokens
   September days are here,
With summer's best of weather,
   And autumn's best of cheer.

But none of all this beauty
   Which floods the earth and air
Is unto me the secret
   Which makes September fair.

'Tis a thing which I remember;
   To name it thrills me yet:
One day of one September
   I never can forget.

—*Helen Hunt Jackson*

The Garden

My heart is a garden tired with autumn,
  Heaped with bending asters and dahlias
    heavy and dark,
In the hazy sunshine, the garden remembers
    April,
  The drench of rains and a snow-drop quick
and clear as a spark;

Daffodils blowing in the cold wind of morning,
  And golden tulips, goblets holding the rain—
The garden will be hushed with snow,
    forgotten soon, forgotten—
  After the stillness, will spring come again?

—*Sara Teasdale*

Indian Summer

At last there came
The sudden fall of frost, when Time
Dreaming through russet September days
Suddenly awoke, and lifting his head, strode
Swiftly forward—made one vast desolating
sweep
Of his scythe, then, rapt with the glory
That burned under his feet, fell dreaming again.
And the clouds soared and the crickets sang
In the brief heat of noon; the corn,
So green, grew sere and dry—
   And in the mist the ploughman's team
   Moved silently, as if in dream—
And it was Indian summer on the plain.

—*Hamlin Garland*

Indian Summer

These are the days when birds come back,
A very few, a bird or two,
To take a backward look.

These are the days when skies put on
The old, old sophistries of June,—
A blue and gold mistake.

Oh, fraud that cannot cheat the bee,
Almost thy plausibility
Induces my belief,

Till ranks of seeds their witness bear,
And softly through the altered air
Hurries a timed leaf!

Oh, sacrament of summer days,
Oh, last communion in the haze,
Permit a child to join,

Thy sacred emblems to partake,
Thy consecrated bread to break,
Taste thine immortal wine!

—*Emily Dickinson*

OCTOBER

October's Bright Blue Weather

O suns and skies and clouds of June,
   And flowers of June together,
Ye cannot rival for one hour
   October's bright blue weather.

When loud the bumblebee makes haste,
   Belated, thriftless vagrant,
And Golden Rod is dying fast,
   And lanes with grapes are fragrant;

When Gentians roll their fringes tight,
   To save them for the morning,
And chestnuts fall from satin burrs
   Without a sound of warning;

When on the ground red apples lie
   In piles like jewels shining,
And redder still on old stone walls
   Are leaves of woodbine twining;

When all the lovely wayside things
    Their white-winged seeds are sowing,
And in the fields, still green and fair,
    Late aftermaths are growing;

When springs run low, and on the brooks,
    In idle golden freighting,
Bright leaves sink noiseless in the hush
    Of woods, for winter waiting;

When comrades seek sweet country haunts,
    By twos and twos together,
And count like misers, hour by hour,
    October's bright blue weather.

O suns and skies and flowers of June,
    Count all your boasts together,
Love loveth best of all the year
    October's bright blue weather.

—*Helen Hunt Jackson*

A Vagabond Song

There is something in the autumn that is native
    to my blood—
Touch of manner, hint of mood;
And my heart is like a rhyme,
With the yellow and the purple and the
    crimson keeping time.
The scarlet of the maples can shake me like a cry
Of bugles going by.
And my lonely spirit thrills
To see the frosty asters like a smoke upon the
    hills.
There is something in October sets the gypsy
    blood astir;
We must rise and follow her,
When from every hill of flame
She calls and calls each vagabond by name.

—*Bliss Carman*

October

Beauty has a tarnished dress,
And a patchwork cloak of cloth
Dipped deep in mournfulness,
Striped like a moth.

Wet grass where it trails
Dyes it green along the hem;
She has seven silver veils
With cracked bells on them.

She is tired of all these—
Grey gauze, translucent lawn;
The broad cloak of Herakles
Is tangled flame and fawn.

Water and light are wearing thin:
She has drawn above her head
The warm enormous lion skin
Rough red and gold.

—*Elinor Morton Wylie*

Maple Leaves

October turned my maple's leaves to gold;
   The most are gone now; here and there one
      lingers:
Soon these will slip from out the twigs' weak
      hold,
   Like coins between a dying miser's fingers.

—*Thomas Bailey Aldrich*

October

October is the treasurer of the year,
   And all the months pay bounty to her store:
The fields and orchards still their tribute bear,
   And fill her brimming coffers more and more.
But she, with youthful lavishness,
Spends all her wealth in gaudy dress,
   And decks herself in garments bold
   Of scarlet, purple, red, and gold.

She heedeth not how swift the hours fly,
   But smiles and sings her happy life along;
She only sees above a shining sky;
   She only hears the breezes' voice in song.
Her garments trail the woodland through,
And gather pearls of early dew
   That sparkle till the roguish Sun
   Creeps up and steals them every one.

But what cares she that jewels should be lost,
　　When all of Nature's bounteous wealth is
　　　hers?
Though princely fortunes may have been their
　　　cost,
　　Not one regret her calm demeanor stirs.
Whole-hearted, happy, careless, free,
She lives her life out joyously,
　　Nor cares when Frost stalks o'er her way
　　And turns her auburn locks to gray.

—*Paul Laurence Dunbar*

Falling Leaves

Leaves fall,
Brown leaves,
Yellow leaves streaked with brown.
They fall,
Flutter,
Fall again.

—Amy Lowell, from "The City of Falling Leaves"

Gathering Leaves

Spades take up leaves
No better than spoons,
And bags full of leaves
Are light as balloons.

I make a great noise
Of rustling all day
Like rabbit and deer
Running away.

But the mountains I raise
Elude my embrace,
Flowing over my arms
And into my face.

I may load and unload
Again and again
Till I fill the whole shed,
And what have I then?

Next to nothing for weight;
And since they grew duller
From contact with earth,
Next to nothing for color.

Next to nothing for use.
But a crop is a crop,
And who's to say where
The harvest shall stop?

—*Robert Frost*

Fall, Leaves, Fall

Fall, leaves, fall; die, flowers, away;
Lengthen night and shorten day;
Every leaf speaks bliss to me
Fluttering from the autumn tree.
I shall smile when wreaths of snow
Blossom where the rose should grow;
I shall sing when night's decay
Ushers in a drearier day.

—*Emily Jane Brontë*

Autumn Days

Yellow, mellow, ripened days,
Sheltered in a golden coating;
O'er the dreamy, listless haze,
White and dainty cloudlets floating;
Winking at the blushing trees,
And the sombre, furrowed fallow;
Smiling at the airy ease
Of the southward-flying swallow.
Sweet and smiling are thy ways,
Beauteous, golden, Autumn days!

Shivering, quivering, tearful days,
Fretfully and sadly weeping;
Dreading still, with anxious gaze,
Icy fetters round thee creeping;
O'er the cheerless, withered plain,
Woefully and hoarsely calling;
Pelting hail and drenching rain
On thy scanty vestments falling.
Sad and mournful are thy ways,
Grieving, wailing, Autumn days!

—*Will Carleton*

Something Told the Wild Geese

Something told the wild geese
   It was time to go.
Though the fields lay golden
   Something whispered,—"Snow."
Leaves were green and stirring,
   Berries, luster-glossed,
But beneath warm feathers
   Something cautioned,—"Frost."
All the sagging orchards
   Steamed with amber spice,
But each wild breast stiffened
   At remembered ice.
Something told the wild geese
   It was time to fly—
Summer sun was on their wings,
   Winter in their cry.

—Rachel Field

Fly Away, Fly Away
Over the Sea

Fly away, fly away over the sea,
Sun-loving swallow, for summer is done;
Come again, come again, come back to me,
Bringing the summer and bringing the sun.

—*Christina Rossetti*

Unharvested

A scent of ripeness from over a wall.
And come to leave the routine road
And look for what had made me stall,
There sure enough was an apple tree
That had eased itself of its summer load,
And of all but its trivial foliage free,
Now breathed as light as a lady's fan.
For there had been an apple fall
As complete as the apple had given man.
The ground was one circle of solid red.

May something go always unharvested!
May much stay out of our stated plan,
Apples or something forgotten and left,
So smelling their sweetness would be no theft.

—*Robert Frost*

When the Frost Is on the Punkin

When the frost is on the punkin and the
    fodder's in the shock,
And you hear the kyouck and gobble of the
    struttin' turkey-cock,
And the clackin' of the guineys, and the cluckin'
    of the hens,
And the rooster's hallylooyer as he tiptoes on
    the fence;
O, it's then's the times a feller is a-feelin' at his
    best,
With the risin' sun to greet him from a night
    of peaceful rest,
As he leaves the house, bareheaded, and goes
    out to feed the stock,
When the frost is on the punkin and the
    fodder's in the shock.

They's something kindo' harty-like about the
    atmusfere
When the heat of summer's over and the
    coolin' fall is here—
Of course we miss the flowers, and the
    blossums on the trees,
And the mumble of the hummin'-birds and
    buzzin' of the bees;
But the air's so appetizin'; and the landscape
    through the haze
Of a crisp and sunny morning of the airly
    autumn days
Is a pictur' that no painter has the colorin' to
    mock—
When the frost is on the punkin and the
    fodder's in the shock.

The husky, rusty russel of the tossels of the
    corn,
And the raspin' of the tangled leaves, as golden
    as the morn;
The stubble in the furries—kindo' lonesome-
    like, but still
A-preachin' sermons to us of the barns they
    growed to fill;
The strawstack in the medder, and the reaper
    in the shed;
The hosses in theyr stalls below—the clover
    overhead!—
O, it sets my hart a-clickin' like the tickin' of a
    clock,
When the frost is on the punkin and the
    fodder's in the shock!

Then your apples all is gethered, and the ones
    a feller keeps
Is poured around the cellar-floor in red and
    yeller heaps;
And your cider-makin's over, and your
    wimmern-folks is through
With their mince and apple-butter, and theyr
    souse and sausage too! . . .
I don't know how to tell it—but ef sich a thing
    could be
As the Angels wantin' boardin', and they'd call
    around on *me*—
I'd want to 'commodate 'em—all the whole-
    indurin' flock—
When the frost is on the punkin and the
    fodder's in the shock!

—*James Whitcomb Riley*

Theme in Yellow

I spot the hills
With yellow balls in autumn.
I light the prairie cornfields
Orange and tawny gold clusters
And I am called pumpkins.
On the last of October
When dusk is fallen
Children join hands
And circle round me
Singing ghost songs
And love to the harvest moon;
I am a jack-o'-lantern
With terrible teeth
And the children know
I am fooling.

—*Carl Sandburg*

from To Autumn

Season of mists and mellow fruitfulness,
    Close bosom-friend of the maturing sun;
Conspiring with him how to load and bless
    With fruit the vines that round the thatch-
        eves run;
To bend with apples the moss'd cottage-trees,
    And fill all fruit with ripeness to the core;
To swell the gourd, and plump the hazel shells
    With a sweet kernel; to set budding more,
And still more, later flowers for the bees,
    Until they think warm days will never cease,
For Summer has o'er-brimm'd their clammy
        cells.

—*John Keats*

A Litany for Hallowe'en

From ghoulies and ghosties,
Long-leggity beasties,
And things that go bump in the night,
Good Lord deliver us.

—*Traditional*

Ghost Sounds

When the moon
rides high,
up overhead—
and I am snug
and warm,
in bed—
in the autumn dark
the ghosts move 'round
making their
mournful,
moaning sound.

I listen to know
when the ghosts
go by.
I hear a wail,
and I hear a sigh.

But I can't quite tell
which I hear
the most—
the wind,
or the wail
of some passing ghost.

—*Anonymous*

Hallowe'en

Tonight is the night
When dead leaves fly
Like witches on switches
Across the sky,
When elf and sprite
Flit through the night
On a moony sheen.

Tonight is the night
When leaves make a sound
Like a gnome in his home
Under the ground,
When spooks and trolls
Creep out of holes
Mossy and green.

Tonight is the night
When pumpkins stare
Through sheaves and leaves
Everywhere,
When ghoul and ghost
And goblin host
Dance round their queen.
It's Hallowee'en.

—*Harry Behn*

Song of the Witches

Double, double toil and trouble;
Fire burn and caldron bubble.
Fillet of a fenny snake,
In the caldron boil and bake;
Eye of newt and toe of frog,
Wool of bat and tongue of dog,
Adder's fork and blind-worm's sting,
Lizard's leg and owlet's wing,
For a charm of powerful trouble,
Like a hell-broth boil and bubble.
Double, double toil and trouble;
Fire burn and caldron bubble.
Cool it with a baboon's blood,
Then the charm is firm and good.

—*William Shakespeare*, Macbeth

NOVEMBER

No!

No sun—no moon!
No morn—no noon—
No dawn—no dusk—no proper time of day—
No sky—no earthly view—
No distance looking blue—
No road—no street—no "t'other side this way"—
No top to any steeple—
No recognitions of familiar people—
No courtesies for showing 'em—
No knowing 'em!
No traveling at all—no locomotion—
No inkling of the way—no notion—
"No go" by land or ocean—
No mail—no post—
No news from any foreign coast—
No park—no ring—no afternoon gentility—
No company—no nobility—

No warmth, no cheerfulness, no healthful ease,
No comfortable feel in any member—
No shade, no shine, no butterflies, no bees,
No fruits, no flowers, no leaves, no birds—
    November!

—*Thomas Hood*

November

The leaves are fading and falling,
  The winds are rough and wild,
The birds have ceased their calling,
  But let me tell you, my child,

Though day by day, as it closes,
  Doth darker and colder grow,
The roots of the bright red roses
  Will keep alive in the snow.

And when the Winter is over,
  The boughs will get new leaves,
The quail come back to the clover,
  And the swallow back to the eaves.

The robin will wear on his bosom
  A vest that is bright and new,
And the loveliest way-side blossom
  Will shine with the sun and dew.

The leaves today are whirling,
    The brooks are dry and dumb,
But let me tell you, my darling,
    The Spring will be sure to come.

There must be rough, cold weather,
    And winds and rains so wild;
Not all good things together
    Come to us here, my child.

So, when some dear joy loses
    Its beauteous summer glow,
Think how the roots of the roses
    Are kept alive in the snow.

—*Alice Cary*

In Flanders Fields

In Flanders fields the poppies blow
Between the crosses row on row,
That mark our place; and in the sky
The larks, still bravely singing, fly
Scarce heard amid the guns below.

We are the Dead. Short days ago
We lived, felt dawn, saw sunset glow,
Loved and were loved, and now we lie
In Flanders fields.

Take up our quarrel with the foe:
To you from failing hands we throw
The torch; be yours to hold it high.
If ye break faith with us who die
We shall not sleep, though poppies grow
In Flanders fields.

—*John McRae*

The Man He Killed

"Had he and I but met
 By some old ancient inn,
We should have sat us down to wet
 Right many a nipperkin!

"But ranged as infantry,
 And staring face to face,
I shot at him as he at me,
 And killed him in his place.

"I shot him dead because—
 Because he was my foe,
Just so: my foe of course he was;
 That's clear enough; although

"He thought he'd 'list, perhaps,
 Off-hand like—just as I—
Was out of work—had sold his traps—
 No other reason why.

"Yes; quaint and curious war is!
    You shoot a fellow down
You'd treat if met where any bar is,
    Or help to half-a-crown."

—*Thomas Hardy*

Down to Sleep

November woods are bare and still;
November days are clear and bright;
Each noon burns up the morning's chill;
The morning's snow is gone by night.
Each day my steps grow slow, grow light,
As through the woods I reverent creep,
Watching all things lie "down to sleep."

I never knew before what beds,
Fragrant to smell, and soft to touch,
The forest sifts and shapes and spreads;
I never knew before how much
Of human sound there is in such
Low tones as through the forest sweep,
When all wild things lie "down to sleep."

Each day I find new coverlids
Tucked in, and more sweet eyes shut tight;
Sometimes the viewless mother bids
Her ferns kneel down full in my sight;
I hear their chorus of "good-night";
And half I smile, and half I weep,
Listening while they lie "down to sleep."

November woods are bare and still;
November days are bright and good;
Life's noon burns up life's morning chill;
Life's night rests feet which long have stood;
Some warm soft bed, in field or wood,
The mother will not fail to keep,
Where we can "lay us down to sleep."

—*Helen Hunt Jackson*

November

The shepherds almost wonder where they dwell,
And the old dog for his right journey stares:
The path leads somewhere, but they cannot tell,
And neighbour meets with neighbour unawares.
The maiden passes close beside her cow,
And wanders on, and thinks her far away;
The ploughman goes unseen behind his plough
And seems to lose his horses half the day.
The lazy mist creeps on in journey slow;
The maidens shout and wonder where they go;
So dull and dark are the November days.
The lazy mist high up the evening curled,
And now the morn quite hides in smoke and haze;
The place we occupy seems all the world.

—*John Clare*

We Plow the Fields and Scatter

We plow the fields, and scatter
The good seed on the land,
But it is fed and watered
By God's almighty hand;
He sends the snow in winter,
The warmth to swell the grain,
The breezes and the sunshine,
And soft refreshing rain.
   All good gifts around us
   Are sent from heaven above,
   Then thank the Lord, O thank the Lord
   For all his love.

—*Matthias Claudius*

A Thanksgiving Poem

The sun hath shed its kindly light,
  Our harvesting is gladly o'er,
Our fields have felt no killing blight,
  Our bins are filled with goodly store.

From pestilence, fire, flood, and sword
  We have been spared by thy decree,
And now with humble hearts, O Lord,
  We come to pay our thanks to thee.

We feel that had our merits been
  The measure of thy gifts to us,
We erring children, born of sin,
  Might not now be rejoicing thus.

No deed of ours hath brought us grace;
  When thou wert nigh our sight was dull,
We hid in trembling from thy face,
  But thou, O God, wert merciful.

Thy mighty hand o'er all the land
    Hath still been open to bestow
Those blessings which our wants demand
    From heaven, whence all blessings flow.

Thou hast, with ever watchful eye,
    Looked down on us with holy care,
And from thy storehouse in the sky
    Hast scattered plenty everywhere.

Then lift we up our songs of praise
    To thee, O Father, good and kind;
To thee we consecrate our days;
    Be thine the temple of each mind.

With incense sweet our thanks ascend;
    Before thy works our powers pall;
Though we should strive years without end,
    We could not thank thee for them all.

—*Paul Laurence Dunbar*

Thanksgiving Day

Over the river, and through the wood,
  To grandfather's house we go;
    The horse knows the way
    To carry the sleigh
  Through the white and drifted snow.

Over the river, and through the wood —
  Oh, how the wind does blow!
    It stings the toes
    And bites the nose
  As over the ground we go.

Over the river and through the wood,
  To have a first-rate play.
    Hear the bells ring,
    "Ting-a-ling-ding!"
  Hurrah for Thanksgiving Day!

Over the river and through the wood
  Trot fast, my dapple-gray!
    Spring over the ground,
    Like a hunting hound!
  For this is Thanksgiving Day.

Over the river and through the wood,
  And straight through the barnyard gate.
    We seem to go
    Extremely slow, —
  It is so hard to wait!

Over the river and through the wood—
  Now grandmother's cap I spy!
    Hurrah for the fun!
    Is the pudding done?
  Hurrah for the pumpkin pie!

—*Lydia Maria Child*

Come, Ye Thankful People, Come

Come, ye thankful people, come,
Raise the song of harvest home:
All is safely gathered in,
Ere the winter storms begin;
God, our Maker, doth provide
For our wants to be supplied;
Come to God's own temple, come,
Raise the song of harvest home.

All the world is God's own field,
Fruit unto His praise to yield;
Wheat and tares together sown,
Unto joy or sorrow grown.
First the blade, and then the ear,
Then the full corn shall appear;
Grant, O harvest Lord, that we
Wholesome grain and pure may be.

For the Lord our God shall come,
And shall take His harvest home;
From His field shall in that day
All offenses purge away,
Give his angels charge at last
In the fire the tares to cast;
But the fruitful ears to store
In His garner evermore.

Even so, Lord, quickly come,
To Thy final harvest home;
Gather thou Thy people in,
Free from sorrow, free from sin;
There, forever purified,
In thy presence to abide:
Come, with all Thine angels, come,
Raise the glorious harvest home. Amen

—*Henry Alford*

Thanks in Old Age

Thanks in old age—thanks ere I go,
For health, the midday sun, the impalpable
    air—for life, mere life,
For precious ever-lingering memories, (of you
    my mother dear—you, father—you,
    brothers, sisters, friends,)
For all my days—not those of peace alone—
    the days of war the same,
For gentle words, caresses, gifts from foreign
    lands,
For shelter, wine and meat—for sweet
    appreciation,
(You distant, dim unknown—or young or
    old—countless, unspecified, readers belov'd,
We never met, and ne'er shall meet—and yet
    our souls embrace, long, close and long;)
For beings, groups, love, deeds, words,
    books—for colors, forms,
For all the brave strong men—devoted, hardy
    men—who've forward sprung in freedom's
    help, all years, all lands,

For braver, stronger, more devoted men—
    (a special laurel ere I go, to life's war's
    chosen ones,
The cannoneers of song and thought—the
    great artillerists—the foremost leaders,
    captains of the soul:)
As soldier from an ended war return'd—
    As traveler out of myriads, to the long
    procession retrospective,
Thanks—joyful thanks!—a soldier's, traveler's
    thanks.

—*Walt Whitman*

DECEMBER

I Heard a Bird Sing

I heard a bird sing
In the dark of December
A magical thing
And sweet to remember:
"We are nearer to Spring
Than we were in September,"
I heard a bird sing
In the dark of December.

—*Oliver Herford*

Blow, Blow, Thou Winter Wind

Blow, blow, thou winter wind,
Thou art not so unkind
As man's ingratitude;
Thy tooth is not so keen
Because thou art not seen,
Although thy breath be rude.
Heigh ho! sing heigh-ho! unto the green holly:
Most friendship is feigning, most loving mere
    folly:
Then, heigh-ho! the holly!
This life is most jolly.

Freeze, freeze, thou bitter sky,
That dost not bite so nigh
As benefits forgot:
Though thou the waters warp,
Thy sting is not so sharp
As friend remember'd not.

Heigh ho! sing heigh ho! unto the green holly:
Most friendship is feigning, most loving mere
folly:
Then, heigh ho! the holly!
This life is most jolly.

—*William Shakespeare*, As You Like It

Dreidel Song

I have a little dreidel,
I made it out of clay,
And when it's dry and ready,
Then dreidel I shall play.

Oh dreidel, dreidel, dreidel,
I made it out of clay;
And when it's dry and ready,
Then dreidel I shall play.

It has a lovely body,
With legs so short and thin,
And when it gets all tired,
It drops and then I win.

Oh dreidel, dreidel, dreidel,
I made it out of clay;
And when it's dry and ready,
Then dreidel I shall play.

—*Anonymous*

Maoz Tzur—Rock of Ages

Rock of Ages, let our song
Praise Your saving power;
You amidst the raging throng
Were our sheltering tower.
Furious they assailed us,
But Your help availed us;
And Your word broke their sword
When our own strength failed us.

Children of the martyr race,
Whether free or fettered,
Praise the Lord for all God's grace,
Where you may be scattered.
Yours the message cheering
That the time is nearing
Which will see all men free,
Tyrants disappearing.

—*M. Jastrow and G. Gottheil*

Christmas Is A-Coming

Christmas is a-coming,
The goose is getting fat,
Please put a penny
In an old man's hat.
If you haven't got a penny,
A ha' penny will do.
If you haven't got a ha' penny,
God bless you!

—*Traditional*

A Visit from St. Nicholas

'Twas the night before Christmas, when all
    through the house
Not a creature was stirring, not even a mouse;
The stockings were hung by the chimney with
    care,
In hopes that St. Nicholas soon would be there.
The children were nestled all snug in their beds,
While visions of sugar-plums danced in their
    heads;
And mamma in her 'kerchief, and I in my cap,
Had just settled our brains for a long winter's
    nap,
When out on the lawn there arose such a clatter,
I sprang from the bed to see what was the matter.
Away to the window I flew like a flash,
Tore open the shutters and threw up the sash.
The moon on the breast of the new-fallen snow
Gave the luster of midday to objects below,
When, what to my wondering eyes should appear,
But a miniature sleigh, and eight tiny reindeer,

With a little old driver, so lively and quick,
I knew in a moment it must be St. Nick.
More rapid than eagles his coursers they came,
And he whistled, and shouted, and called them
by name;
"Now, DASHER! now, DANCER! now,
PRANCER and VIXEN!
On, COMET! on, CUPID! on, DONDER and
BLITZEN!
To the top of the porch! to the top of the wall!
Now dash away! dash away! dash away all!"
As dry leaves that before the wild hurricane fly,
When they meet with an obstacle, mount to the
sky,
So up to the housetop the coursers they flew,
With the sleigh full of toys, and St. Nicholas too.
And then, in a twinkling, I heard on the roof
The prancing and pawing of each little hoof.
As I drew in my head, and was turning around,
Down the chimney St. Nicholas came with a
bound.

He was dressed all in fur, from his head to his
    foot,
And his clothes were all covered with ashes and
    soot;
A bundle of toys he had flung on his back,
And he looked like a peddler just opening his
    pack.
His eyes—how they twinkled! his dimples how
    merry!
His cheeks were like roses, his nose like a cherry!
His droll little mouth was drawn up like a bow,
And the beard of his chin was as white as the
    snow;
The stump of a pipe he held tight in his teeth,
And the smoke it encircled his head like a wreath;
He had a broad face and a little round belly
That shook, when he laughed, like a bowlful of
    jelly.

He was chubby and plump, a right jolly old elf,
And I laughed when I saw him, in spite of
    myself;
A wink of his eye and a twist of his head,
Soon gave me to know I had nothing to dread;
He spoke not a word, but went straight to his
    work,
And filled all the stockings; then turned with a
    jerk,
And laying his finger aside of his nose
And giving a nod, up the chimney he rose;
He sprang to his sleigh, to his team gave a
    whistle,
And away they all flew like the down of a thistle.
But I heard him exclaim, ere he drove out of
    sight,
"Happy Christmas to all, and to all a good night."

—*Clement Clarke Moore*

I Heard the Bells on Christmas Day

I heard the bells on Christmas Day
Their old, familiar carols play,
  And wild and sweet
  The words repeat
Of peace on earth, good-will to men!

And thought how, as the day had come,
The belfries of all Christendom
  Had rolled along
  The unbroken song
Of peace on earth, good-will to men!

Till, ringing, singing on its way,
The world revolved from night to day,
  A voice, a chime,
  A chant sublime
Of peace on earth, good-will to men!

Then from each black, accursed mouth
The cannon thundered in the South,
    And with the sound
    The carols drowned
Of peace on earth, good-will to men!

It was as if an earthquake rent
The hearth stones of a continent,
    And made forlorn
    The households born
Of peace on earth, good-will to men!

And in despair I bowed my head;
"There is no peace on earth," I said;
    "For hate is strong,
    And mocks the song
Of peace on earth, good-will to men!"

Then pealed the bells more loud and deep:
"God is not dead, nor doth He sleep!
    The Wrong shall fail,
    The Right prevail,
With peace on earth, good-will to men!"

—*Henry Wadsworth Longfellow*

Christmas Eve

Christmas hath darkness
Brighter than the blazing noon,
Christmas hath a chillness
Warmer than the heat of June,
Christmas hath a beauty
Lovelier than the world can show:
For Christmas bringeth Jesus,
Brought for us so low.

Earth, strike up your music,
Birds that sing and bells that ring;
Heaven hath answering music
For all Angels soon to sing:
Earth, put on your whitest
Bridal robe of spotless snow:
For Christmas bringeth Jesus,
Brought for us so low.

—*Christina Rossetti*

Christ's Nativity

Awake, glad heart! get up and sing!
It is the birth-day of thy King.
   Awake! awake!
   The Sun doth shake
Light from his locks, and all the way
Breathing perfumes, doth spice the day.

Awake, awake! hark how th' wood rings;
Winds whisper, and the busy springs
   A concert make;
   Awake! awake!
Man is their high-priest, and should rise
To offer up the sacrifice.

I would I were some bird, or star,
Flutt'ring in woods, or lifted far
   Above this inn
   And road of sin!
Then either star or bird should be
Shining or singing still to Thee.

I would I had in my best part
Fit rooms for thee! or that my heart
   Were so clean as
   Thy manger was!
But I am all filth, and obscene;
Yet, if Thou wilt, Thou canst make clean.

Sweet Jesu! will then; Let no more
This leper haunt and soil Thy door!
   Cure him, ease him,
   O release him!
And let once more, by mystic birth,
The Lord of life be born in earth.

—*Henry Vaughan*

While Shepherds Watched Their Flocks

While shepherds watched their flocks by night,
　All seated on the ground,
The angel of the Lord came down,
　And glory shone around.

"Fear not," said he,—for mighty dread
　Had seized their troubled mind—
"Glad tidings of great joy I bring
　To you and all mankind.

"To you, in David's town, this day
　Is born, of David's line,
The Saviour, who is Christ the Lord;
　And this shall be the sign:

"The heavenly babe you there shall find
　To human view displayed,
All meanly wrapped in swathing bands,
　And in a manger laid."

Thus spake the seraph; and forthwith
  Appeared a shining throng
Of angels, praising God, and thus
  Addressed their joyful song:

"All glory be to God on high,
  And to the earth be peace:
Good-will henceforth from heaven to men
  Begin and never cease!"

—*Nahum Tate*

Christmas Carol

The kings they came from out the south,
   All dressed in ermine fine,
They bore Him gold and chrysoprase,
   And gifts of precious wine.

The shepherds came from out the north,
   Their coats were brown and old,
They brought Him little new-born lambs—
   They had not any gold.

The wise-men came from out the east,
   And they were wrapped in white;
The star that led them all the way
   Did glorify the night.

The angels came from heaven high,
   And they were clad with wings;
And lo, they brought a joyful song
   The host of heaven sings.

The kings they knocked upon the door,
  The wise-men entered in,
The shepherds followed after them
  To hear the song begin.

And Mary held the little child
  And sat upon the ground;
She looked up, she looked down,
  She looked all around.

The angels sang thro' all the night
  Until the rising sun,
But little Jesus fell asleep
  Before the song was done.

—*Sara Teasdale*

Passing of the Old Year

Ah! the year is slowly dying,
And the wind in tree-top sighing,
Chant his requiem.
Thick and fast the leaves are falling,
High in air wild birds are calling,
Nature's solemn hymn.

—*Mary Weston Fordham*

The Old Year

The Old Year's gone away
   To nothingness and night:
We cannot find him all the day
   Nor hear him in the night:
He left no footstep, mark or place
   In either shade or sun:
The last year he'd a neighbour's face,
   In this he's known by none.

All nothing everywhere:
   Mists we on mornings see
Have more of substance when they're here
   And more of form than he.
He was a friend by every fire,
   In every cot and hall—
A guest to every heart's desire,
   And now he's nought at all.

Old papers thrown away,
   Old garments cast aside,
The talk of yesterday,
   All things identified;
But times once torn away
   No voices can recall:
The eve of New Year's Day
   Left the Old Year lost to all.

—*John Clare*

Ring Out, Wild Bells

Ring out, wild bells, to the wild sky,
 The flying cloud, the frosty light:
 The year is dying in the night;
Ring out, wild bells, and let him die.

Ring out the old, ring in the new,
 Ring, happy bells, across the snow:
 The year is going, let him go;
Ring out the false, ring in the true.

—*Alfred, Lord Tennyson*

Auld Lang Syne

Should auld acquaintance be forgot,
And never brought to mind?
Should auld acquaintance be forgot,
And auld lang syne?
> *For auld lang syne, my dear,*
> *For auld lang syne,*
> *We'll take a cup of kindness yet,*
> *For auld lang syne.*

—*Traditional*

AFTERWORD

Holidays

The holiest of all holidays are those
Kept by ourselves in silence and apart;
The secret anniversaries of the heart,
When the full river of feeling overflows;—
The happy days unclouded to their close;
The sudden joys that out of darkness start
As flames from ashes; swift desires that dart
Like swallows singing down each wind that
    blows.
White as the gleam of a receding sail,
White as a cloud that floats and fades in air,
White as the whitest lily on a stream,
These tender memories are;—a fairy tale
Of some enchanted land we know not where,
But lovely as a landscape in a dream.

—*Henry Wadsworth Longfellow*

PERMISSIONS ACKNOWLEDGMENTS

INDEX OF AUTHORS

INDEX OF TITLES ～

INDEX OF FIRST LINES ᮝ